W9-AHA-755

OUR
GRE★T
STATES

WHAT'S GREAT ABOUT
FLORIDA?

✳ Mary Meinking

⌐ LERNER PUBLICATIONS COMPANY ✳ MINNEAPOLIS

CONTENTS

Content Consultant: John Sacher, Chair, Department of History, University of Central Florida

Lerner Publications Company
A division of Lerner Publishing Group, Inc.
241 First Avenue North
Minneapolis, MN 55401 USA

For reading levels and more information, look up this title at www.lernerbooks.com.

Main body text set in ITC Franklin Gothic Std Book Condensed 12/15.
Typeface provided by Adobe Systems.

Library of Congress Cataloging-in-Publication Data

Meinking, Mary.
    What's great about Florida? / by Mary Meinking.
        pages cm. — (Our great states)
        Includes index.
    ISBN 978-1-4677-3391-5 (lib. bdg. : alk. paper)
    ISBN 978-1-4677-4708-0 (eBook)
    1. Florida—Juvenile literature. I. Title.
F311.3.M45 2015
975.9—dc23   2013048344

Manufactured in the United States of America
1 – PC – 7/15/14

FLORIDA Welcomes You!

Florida is one of the world's top places to visit. It's easy to see why. Florida is known for its year-round warm weather. But that's not all. Tourists of all ages enjoy Florida's many theme parks. People also come for the state's nature and history. From the Panhandle to the Keys, there's so much to see and do in the Sunshine State! Keep reading to learn the top ten things that make Florida great!

ALABAMA

Britton Hill

Pensacola

Gulf Breeze

GEORGIA

● Tallahassee

Apalachicola River

Saint Marys River

Okefenokee Swamp

Jacksonville ●

Suwannee River

Saint Johns River

ATLANTIC OCEAN

GULF OF MEXICO

Miles
0   20   40   60

0   40   80
Kilometers

Withlacoochee River

Orlando ●

Tampa ●

Saint Petersburg

N

Lake Okeechobee

Caloosahatchee River

Cape Coral ●

Explore Florida's beaches and all the places in between! Just turn the page to find out all about the SUNSHINE STATE. >

Fort Lauderdale ●

Hialeah ●
● Miami

Everglades National Park

Key West ●

ORLANDO THEME PARKS

> Orlando is a perfect first stop for a trip to Florida. It is home to some of the country's best-known theme parks. In fact, there are eight theme parks in Orlando!

Walt Disney World has some of Orlando's most popular parks. Meet your favorite Disney characters at Magic Kingdom. Disney's Hollywood Studios brings movies to life. Tour countries around the world at Epcot. Lions, giraffes, and zebras roam the grounds at Disney's Animal Kingdom.

Next, head to Universal Orlando Resort. It has two theme parks. Universal Studios Florida and Universal's Islands of Adventure are movie-themed parks. Don't miss The Wizarding World of Harry Potter attraction. You'll feel like you're part of the Harry Potter books and movies!

Do you like learning about marine life? You might enjoy SeaWorld and Discovery Cove. You'll get an up-close look at dolphins, killer whales, and more!

The Wizarding World of Harry Potter lets visitors feel as though they are part of the Harry Potter novels, written by author J. K. Rowling.

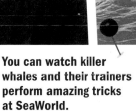

You can watch killer whales and their trainers perform amazing tricks at SeaWorld.

SAINT AUGUSTINE

> Feel history come to life at Saint Augustine. This is the oldest continuously settled city in the United States. Saint Augustine is on Florida's northeast coast. Spanish explorers settled here in 1565. People have occupied the area ever since.

Castillo de San Marcos National Monument is the oldest stone fort in the United States. Scramble up to the gun deck. Hear the cannons *boom* when fired. Many of the fort's workers dress in costumes from the 1600s. They talk about what life was like at the fort.

Visiting the Colonial Quarter is like stepping back in time. Be part of a musket drill. Watch blacksmiths bend metal. You can even make a leather bracelet, and dig for buried artifacts.

You may be thirsty after your time travel. Stop at Ponce de León's Fountain of Youth Archeological Park. Here, you can have a cool drink of spring water. If you believe the legend, the water will keep you young forever.

JUAN PONCE DE LEÓN

In 1513, Spanish explorer Juan Ponce de León came to Florida. He and his three ships probably landed near what is now Cape Canaveral. He was searching for gold and new land for Spain. He landed around the Easter holiday. So he named the land Florida or Pascua Florida. This Spanish phrase describes an Easter celebration.

Costumed workers demonstrate how to load the cannons at Castillo de San Marcos National Monument.

THE PANHANDLE

> The Florida Panhandle is a must-see stop on your Florida trip. The Panhandle is the strip of land that makes up northwestern Florida. While there, check out Pensacola.

Don't miss Pensacola's National Naval Aviation Museum. More than 150 famous aircrafts are housed there. You can watch the Blue Angels practice tricks as they fly through the air. These navy pilots are some of the best flyers in the world.

The museum is free to visit. Inside, you can get behind the controls of a flight simulator. You'll feel as though you're riding with the Blue Angels in the IMAX theater. Try out dozens of hands-on flight experiments. Then step outside. Here, you can take the bus tour past about forty aircraft.

Once the museum closes, head across the bay to Gulf Breeze. Keep your eyes to the sky. Gulf Breeze has been the site of more UFO sightings than any other place east of the Mississippi River. Maybe you'll spot a UFO above the water!

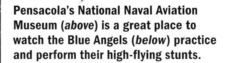

Pensacola's National Naval Aviation Museum (*above*) is a great place to watch the Blue Angels (*below*) practice and perform their high-flying stunts.

DAYTONA INTERNATIONAL SPEEDWAY

> It's time to rev your engines at Daytona International Speedway. All types of car races are held here. On race days, watch the cars zip around the Speedway's 2.5-mile (4-kilometer) track. The most famous race is NASCAR's Daytona 500. It takes place each year in February. Watch drivers circle the track two hundred times.

On non-race days, take a tour of the Speedway. You'll see behind the scenes at the track, the pit road, and victory lane. Buckle up, and try zooming around the track in a real race car. You can ride shotgun with a professional driver. You may reach speeds up to 160 miles (258 km) per hour. Better hang on tight!

Daytona International Speedway is the home of the Daytona 500 and many other exciting car races.

After a day at the racetrack, hit Daytona's famous beach on the Atlantic Ocean for some fun in the sun.

KENNEDY SPACE CENTER

> Have you ever dreamed of being an astronaut? Then blast off at Kennedy Space Center! It is on the Atlantic coast near Cape Canaveral. This is where all manned rockets blasted off to the moon. Expeditions to the International Space Station also launched here. Rockets still launch from the Kennedy Space Center. Maybe you'll get to see one take off!

More than 1.5 million guests visit the Kennedy Space Center each year. Visitors can explore the past, present, and future of the US space program. The space shuttle *Atlantis* is on display at the center. You can take a walk through a space shuttle model. Then ride the simulator to learn what a shuttle takeoff feels like. Lucky visitors may meet a real NASA astronaut. You can touch a moon rock at the Apollo/Saturn V Center. Then kick back and watch an IMAX movie about space exploration.

The *Saturn V* rocket at the Kennedy Space Center is the largest rocket ever flown.

THE SPACE SHUTTLE PROGRAM

From 1962 until 2011, thousands of people worked for the space shuttle program. They spent their money on new cars, tools, and homes. This helped small towns in Florida grow. Tourists flocked to Cape Canaveral to watch rocket launches. Then NASA canceled the program in 2011. Many people lost their jobs. This hurt Florida's economy.

BASEBALL SPRING TRAINING

> Florida's mild weather makes it a great place for winter baseball. Come watch your favorite baseball teams play from late February through March. Many Major League Baseball (MLB) teams get a head start on their seasons here. The MLB has held spring training camps in Florida for more than 125 years. Fifteen MLB teams train across the state. They are part of what is known as the Grapefruit League. The teams play one another to practice for the baseball season.

On average, 1.6 million baseball fans attend Florida's spring training games each year. The stadiums are small. This lets you get close to your favorite players. Bring your glove to catch a foul ball. Hang out after the games to get players' autographs. Maybe you can get your picture with them.

More fans go to Boston Red Sox and New York Yankees spring training games than any other teams' games. The Sox play in Fort Myers. The Yankees play in Tampa.

The New York Yankees are one of the Grapefruit League's most popular teams to watch at spring training.

FLORIDA'S WEATHER

Florida averages temperatures of 61 to 66°F (16 to 19°C) during spring training. The balmy weather draws non-baseball fans too. Many people head south to the Sunshine State. They want to leave the winter cold. This helps make tourism Florida's most important industry. Agriculture also is an important Florida industry. Florida's warm weather gives farmers a long growing season. Many fruits and vegetables grow here year-round.

SANIBEL ISLAND

> Florida is known for its beaches. If you like to collect shells, there's no better beach than on Sanibel Island. This island juts out into the Gulf of Mexico. You can find some of the world's most beautiful seashells here. In fact, it's one of the three best shelling beaches on Earth.

The best time to find the most shells is around low tide. Wear wave shoes or flip-flops. Be sure to bring a box for your treasures. You might even find a sand dollar.

While you're on the island, also plan a stop at the Bailey-Matthews Shell Museum. Here you can see thousands of shells from around the world. You can see fossils too. Don't miss the displays in the Children's Learning Lab. Try your hand at the lab's shell games. Touch creatures in the live shell tank.

After a long day of shelling, relax on the beach. You can watch the sunset.

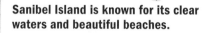
Sanibel Island is known for its clear waters and beautiful beaches.

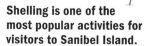
Shelling is one of the most popular activities for visitors to Sanibel Island.

ORANGE GROVES

> Florida is famous for its fruit. The state grows more than half the nation's citrus fruits. These include grapefruit, lemons, oranges, and tangerines. Pick your own fruit at one of Florida's many citrus groves. Stop by Showcase of Citrus near Orlando. There, you can pick your own oranges to take home. Hop on the grove's swamp buggy. It will show you around the orange grove and the nearby forest.

For a real citrus treat, visit Al's Family Farms in Fort Pierce. There, you'll learn about what it takes to be an orange farmer. Learn how to wash oranges. Take a tour of the packinghouse. You'll get to see how oranges are packed.

Pretend you're a farmer at Al's O.J. Corral. You can pick oranges and walk through the mini citrus grove. Race oranges using old-fashioned water pumps. Spray the oranges to see which ones move the fastest. Then see if you can find your way out of the citrus maze. Finish off your visit with a glass of fresh-squeezed orange juice.

Many of Florida's orange groves give you the chance to learn how citrus farmers grow and harvest their crops. You can also pick your own fruit to take home.

EVERGLADES NATIONAL PARK

> Everglades National Park is one of the strangest places on Earth. It is a swampy area in southern Florida. It covers more than 1.5 million acres (607,000 hectares). It's sometimes called a river of grass.

The Everglades are a wildlife haven. They are home to the endangered Florida panther. Alligators and manatees also make their home in the swampland. More than three hundred species of birds fly between the tall grasses.

The best way to see wildlife up close is on the water. From Everglades City, you can ride on a swamp buggy or a fan boat. Or you can paddle a kayak or a canoe.

On dry land, hike the Shark Valley's trail. You can take it to the observation tower. You'll pass through tall saw grass fields. Be on the lookout for wildlife. And don't forget your mosquito spray!

On your hike, you may catch a whiff of the skunk ape. This giant creature is 7 feet (2.1 meters) tall. It's said to look like Bigfoot. You'll know it by its skunky smell.

THE SEMINOLES

In the 1700s, three major American Indian groups called Florida home. They were the Creeks, the Yuchis, and the Yamassees. Some of them moved to Florida from southern Georgia. In the 1770s, all Florida American Indians became known as the Seminoles. By the early 1800s, European settlers moved onto Seminole land. Three Seminole Wars broke out. The US government tried to force the Seminoles to move to Oklahoma. Approximately three hundred Seminoles hid in the Everglades. More than two thousand Seminoles still live on six reservations across Florida.

Alligators are just one of the many types of wildlife you might see on a visit to Everglades National Park.

FLORIDA KEYS

> End your trip to Florida by heading as far south as you can go. The Florida Keys is a chain of islands. It is more than 150 miles (241 km) long. You'll find plenty to see and do both above and below the clear ocean waters.

Would you like to swim with dolphins? The Dolphin Research Center in Marathon is the place to do it. Spend a day with a dolphin trainer. Take a plunge in a pool with dolphins. You can even work with a dolphin to paint a T-shirt.

Then visit the John Pennekamp Coral Reef State Park near Key Largo. This was the first underwater park in the United States. It is a great place to see marine life in nature. You'll have fun exploring this 70-nautical-square-mile (240 sq. km) reef. Snorkel among the fish. Or stay high and dry in a glass-bottom boat.

In Key West, you can see real sunken treasure. The Mel Fisher Maritime Museum is home to many riches. They came from sunken ships. See sparkling emeralds and diamonds. You even can see an 8.5-foot-long (2.6 m) gold chain.

YOUR TOP TEN!

You've just read about ten fun things to do and see in Florida. Now it's your turn! Imagine you're planning a trip to Florida. What would your top ten list include? What places in Florida would you most like to see? Grab a sheet of paper and jot down your Florida top ten list. You can make it into a book. Just add drawings or pictures from the Internet.

The southern tip of Key West is the southernmost point in the continental United States. You can stand only 90 miles (145 km) from Cuba!

John Pennekamp Coral Reef State Park is full of colorful fish and other marine life.

25

FLORIDA BY MAP

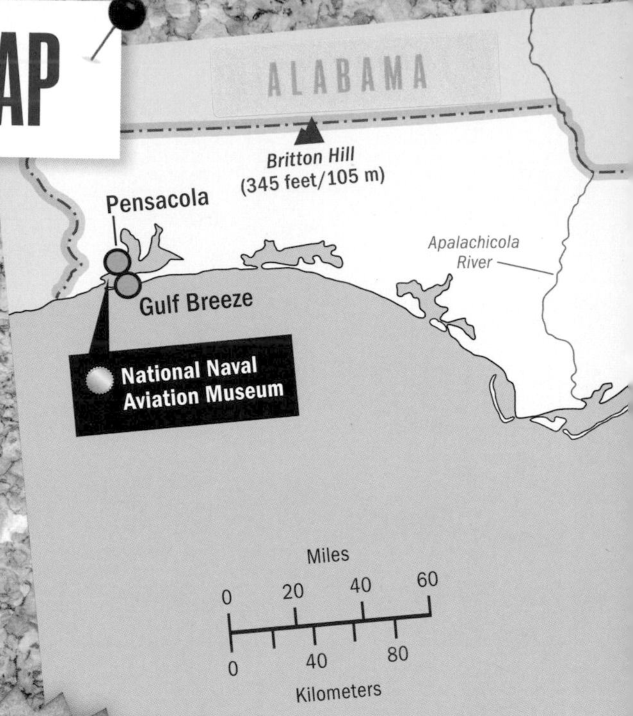

ALABAMA

▲ Britton Hill
(345 feet/105 m)

Pensacola

Apalachicola
River

Gulf Breeze

National Naval
Aviation Museum

> MAP KEY

⬟ Capital city

◯ City

◉ Point of interest

▲ Highest elevation

–·– State border

◆ Baseball spring
training stadiums

Miles

0   20   40   60

0   40   80

Kilometers

GREAT SEAL OF THE STATE OF FLORIDA

IN GOD WE TRUST

Visit www.lerneresource.com to learn
more about the state flag of Florida.

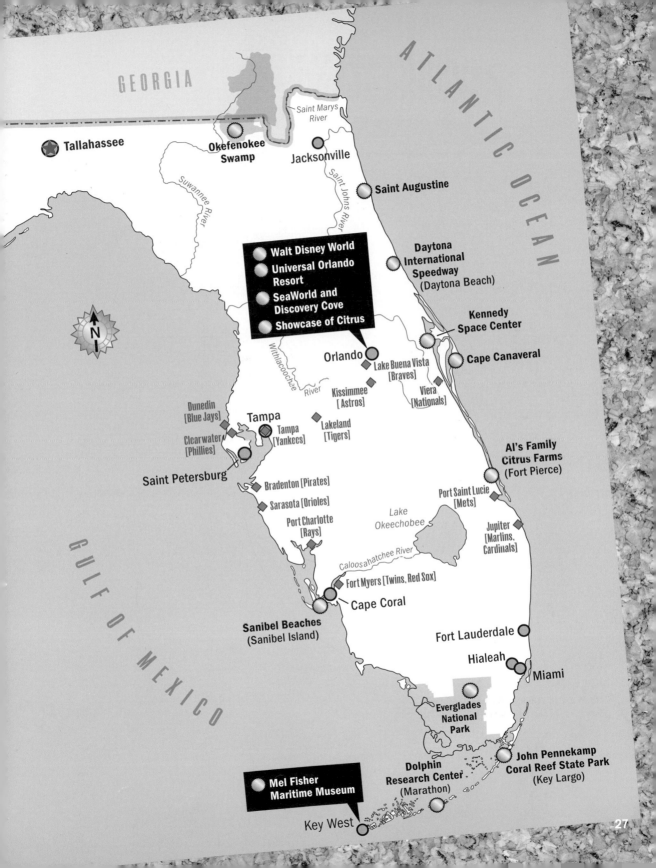

GEORGIA

ATLANTIC OCEAN

Saint Marys River

Tallahassee

Okefenokee Swamp

Jacksonville

Suwannee River

Saint Johns River

Saint Augustine

Walt Disney World

Universal Orlando Resort

SeaWorld and Discovery Cove

Showcase of Citrus

Daytona International Speedway (Daytona Beach)

Kennedy Space Center

Orlando

Lake Buena Vista [Braves]

Cape Canaveral

Withlacoochee River

Kissimmee [Astros]

Viera [Nationals]

N

Dunedin [Blue Jays]

Tampa

Tampa [Yankees]

Lakeland [Tigers]

Clearwater [Phillies]

Saint Petersburg

Al's Family Citrus Farms (Fort Pierce)

Bradenton [Pirates]

Sarasota [Orioles]

Port Saint Lucie [Mets]

Lake Okeechobee

Port Charlotte [Rays]

Jupiter [Marlins, Cardinals]

Caloosahatchee River

Fort Myers [Twins, Red Sox]

Cape Coral

Sanibel Beaches (Sanibel Island)

Fort Lauderdale

Hialeah

Miami

Everglades National Park

John Pennekamp Coral Reef State Park (Key Largo)

GULF OF MEXICO

Mel Fisher Maritime Museum

Dolphin Research Center (Marathon)

Key West

27

FLORIDA FACTS

NICKNAME: Sunshine State

SONG: "The Swanee River (Old Folks at Home)" by Stephen C. Foster

MOTTO: "In God We Trust"

FLOWER: orange blossom

TREE: sabal palm

BIRD: northern mockingbird

ANIMAL: Florida panther

FOOD: orange juice

DATE AND RANK OF STATEHOOD: March 3, 1845; the 27th state

CAPITAL: Tallahassee

AREA: 58,976 square miles (152,747 sq. km)

AVERAGE JANUARY TEMPERATURE: 59.4°F (15.2°C)

AVERAGE JULY TEMPERATURE: 81.3°F (27.4°C)

POPULATION AND RANK: 19,317,568; 4th (2012)

MAJOR CITIES AND POPULATIONS: Jacksonville (836,507), Miami (413,892), Tampa (347,645), Orlando (249,562), Saint Petersburg (246,541)

NUMBER OF US CONGRESS MEMBERS: 27 representatives, 2 senators

NUMBER OF ELECTORAL VOTES: 29

NATURAL RESOURCES: clay, crushed stone, limestone, lumber, peat, phosphate rock, staurolite, zirconium

AGRICULTURAL PRODUCTS: grapefruit, oranges, peanuts, potatoes, sugarcane, tangerines, other fruits and vegetables

MANUFACTURED GOODS: chemicals, computer and electronic equipment, machinery, paper, plastics, rubber products, tobacco products, transportation equipment

STATE HOLIDAYS AND CELEBRATIONS: Pascua Florida Day

GLOSSARY

agriculture: farming

artifact: an object used in the past that was made by humans

blacksmith: a person who makes and fixes objects by heating and shaping iron

economy: the system in which goods are produced, bought, and sold in a place

endangered: threatened with extinction

fossil: the ancient remains of a plant or animal preserved in rock

legend: a story from the past that can't be proven true

musket: an old-fashioned gun once used by soldiers

NASA: the National Aeronautics and Space Administration, a US government agency that works to improve our understanding of space

reservation: land set aside by the government for American Indians to live on

simulator: a machine used to imitate what an object or action looks or feels like

UFO: unidentified flying object, or an object some people believe is a spaceship from another planet

LERNER
SOURCE™

Expand learning beyond the printed book. Download free, complementary educational resources for this book from our website, www.lerneresource.com.

FURTHER INFORMATION

Annino, J. G. *She Sang Promise: The Story of Betty Mae Jumper, Seminole Tribal Leader*. Washington, DC: National Geographic Children's Books, 2010. Learn how Betty Mae Jumper grew up in the Everglades and became the country's first female elected tribal leader.

The Bailey-Matthews Shell Museum: Kid's Stuff
http://shellmuseum.org/education/kids.cfm
This website features shell games and offers a free children's admission ticket to the museum.

Bullard, Lisa. *The Everglades*. Minneapolis: Lerner Publications, 2010. Read about the Everglades, including the animals that live there, how people use it, and how we can protect this huge swamp.

Dolphin Research Center: Just for Kids
http://www.dolphins.org/just_for_kids
Learn about marine mammals, play games at the Kids Game Zone, and learn how you can help protect dolphins at Conservation Corner.

Florida Department of State Division of Historical Resources: Florida Kids Web Site
http://flheritage.com/kids
Learn about Florida state symbols, Florida history, Seminole history, and other fun facts.

Sullivan, Ann. *Florida: The Sunshine State*. New York: AV2 by Weigl, 2012. This book is full of information about Florida, including geography, sports, and history.

INDEX

PHOTO ACKNOWLEDGMENTS

The images in this book are used with the permission of: © Cheryl Casey/Shutterstock Images, p. 1; © Katherine Welles/Thinkstock, p. 4; © Laura Westlund/Independent Picture Service, pp. 5 (top), 26–27; © Juho Ruohola/Thinkstock, p. 5 (bottom); © Blaine Harrington III/Corbis, pp. 6–7; © Kike Calvo/AP Images, p. 7 (top); © Mike Liu/Shutterstock Images, p. 7 (bottom); © Getty Images/Thinkstock, pp. 8, 8–9; © Jorg Hackemann/Shutterstock, p. 9; © digidreamgrafix/Shutterstock Images, pp. 10–11; © Steven Frame/Shutterstock Images, p. 11 (top); © Cheryl Casey/Shutterstock Images, p. 11 (bottom); © Action Sports Photography/Shutterstock Images, pp. 12–13; © Katherine Welles/Shutterstock Images, p. 13 (top); © Chris Parypa Photography/Shutterstock Images, p. 13 (bottom); © Nigel Worrall/Demotix/Corbis, pp. 14–15; © Samot/Shutterstock Images, p. 15 (left); © Purestock/Shutterstock Images, p. 15 (right); © Evan Meyer/Shutterstock Images, pp. 16–17; © Cliff Welch/Icon SMI, p. 17 (left); © Rudy Umans/Shutterstock Images, p. 17 (right); © planet5D LLC/Shutterstock Images, pp. 18–19; © sportsrock/iStockphoto, p. 19 (top); © Mitch Aunger/Thinkstock, p. 19 (bottom); © Jason Patrick Ross/Shutterstock Images, pp. 20–21; © age fotostock/SuperStock, p. 21 (top); © Nimazi/Shutterstock Images, p. 21 (bottom); Daniel Rice & James G. Clark/Library of Congress (LC-USZC4-2380), p. 22; © Hoberman Collection/Glow Images, p. 22-23; © Clark Wheeler/Thinkstock, p. 23; © Bertl123/Shutterstock Images, pp. 24–25; © Andrew Jalbert/Thinkstock, p. 25 (left); © Maisna/Shutterstock Images, p. 25 (right); © Atlaspix/Shutterstock Images, p. 26; © Judi Parkinson/Thinkstock, p. 29 (top); © forestpath/Shutterstock Images, p. 29 (middle top); © bephotographers/Thinkstock, p. 29 (middle bottom); © happyjones/Thinkstock, p. 29 (bottom).

Cover: © Valentin Armianu/Dreamstime.com (Disneyworld); © Flick47/Shutterstock.com, front cove (oranges); © Sorbis/Shutterstock.com, (alligator); © Laura Westlund/Independent Picture Service (map); © iStockphoto.com/fpm (seal); © iStockphoto.com/vicm (pushpins); © iStockphoto.com/benz190 (cork board)